Civil War Wa

SAVANNAH

David D'Arcy & Ben Mammina

4880 Lower Valley Road, Atglen, PA 19310 USA

Published by Schiffer Publishing Ltd.
4880 Lower Valley Road
Atglen, PA 19310
Phone: (610) 593-1777; Fax: (610) 593-2002
E-mail: Info@schifferbooks.com

For the largest selection of fine reference books on this and related subjects, please visit our
web site at **www.schifferbooks.com**
We are always looking for people to write books on new and related subjects. If you have an
idea for a book please contact us at the above address.

This book may be purchased from the publisher.
Include $3.95 for shipping.
Please try your bookstore first.
You may write for a free catalog.

In Europe, Schiffer books are distributed by
Bushwood Books
6 Marksbury Ave.
Kew Gardens
Surrey TW9 4JF England
Phone: 44 (0) 20 8392-8585; Fax: 44 (0) 20 8392-9876
E-mail: info@bushwoodbooks.co.uk
Website: www.bushwoodbooks.co.uk
Free postage in the U.K., Europe; air mail at cost.

Library of Congress Cataloging-in-Publication Data

D'Arcy, David.
  Civil War walking tours of Savannah / David D'Arcy & Ben Mammina.
    p. cm.
  ISBN 0-7643-2537-X (pbk.)
  1. Savannah (Ga.)—Tours. 2. Savannah (Ga.)—Buildings, structures, etc.—Guidebooks.
3. Historic buildings—Georgia—Savannah—Guidebooks 4. Historic sites—Georgia—
Savannah—Guidebooks. 5. Savannah (Ga.)—History—19th century. I. Mammina, Ben. II.
Title.

F294.S2D37 2006
975.8'724—dc22

                              2006017054

Cover and book designed by: Bruce Waters
Type set in Americana XBd BT/Zurich BT

ISBN: 0-7643-2537-X
Printed in China

Dedication

For Jennifer, my love, whose love of me and Savannah taught me patience and opened my eyes to a Savannah I never relished.

For my parents, allowing me to visit some of those Civil War sites that are very special to me.

Acknowledgments

I would first like to thank Ben Mammina for taking on this project. His vision allowed for a different perspective of what we could bring out in our photographs. Ben was also a great friend, standing by me during the ups and downs that I went through while putting this book together.

Next I would like to thank Savannah Walks. Also, thanks to Katherine Britton Elliot for proofreading the manuscript for grammar and clarity. Katherine was very supportive of me during this process. Michael Dow Harris was great in comparing stories with me and helping me find additional sources. David Rousseau helped me find Schiffer Publishing and compared notes as his writing project evolved. Hilton Swing, for allowing me to use his library to help research the book. Brandi Kincaid, for being objective and giving me advice through the experience.

Gratitude also goes out to Jewell Anderson for answering all my questions while researching at the Georgia Historical Society. I would also like to thank Lydia Mortonson of the Coastal Heritage Society for copying images from their collection to help illustrate the book.

The staff at Fort Jackson is greatly appreciated for allowing me to use their library and photographing their living history events.

Additional thanks goes out to Tally Kirkland, former Chief Ranger at Fort Pulaski, and to current Chief Ranger, June Davisfruto, for their wealth of information and use of images from their collections.

Daniel Brown, superintendent at Fort McAllister, and his staff were available to me. Photographs from their living history programs were also a great help.

Chica Arndt of the Savannah-Ogeechee Canal and Nature Center helped with the historical information on the canal and its importance to the Confederate defenses in December 1864.

Dana Cole, of the Green-Meldrim House, allowed me to peer into the life of Charles Green and Sherman's occupation of the residence.

Tommy Groms, from the Round House Museum, was helpful in allowing me to pry into the history of the repair shops that were built in the early 1850s.

Karen Wortham, historian of the First African Baptist Church, gave me a different perspective on slavery in Savannah.

All contributed and it would not have been possible to complete the work without all the help I received from these fine people.

Contents

Savannah at the start of the Civil War. *Courtesy of the Coastal Heritage Society and Savannah History Museum.*

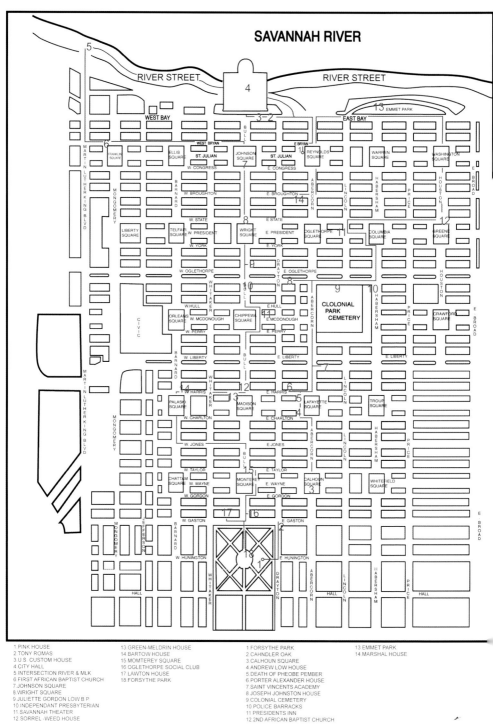

SAVANNAH RIVER

RIVER STREET

RIVER STREET

EMMET PARK

WEST BAY

EAST BAY

WEST BRYAN

E BRYAN

FRANKLIN
SQUARE

ELLIS
SQUARE

ST. JULIAN

JOHNSON
SQUARE

ST. JULIAN

REYNOLDS
SQUARE

WARREN
SQUARE

WASHINGTON
SQUARE

W. CONGRESS

E. CONGRESS

W. BROUGHTON

E. BROUGHTON

W. STATE

E STATE

LIBERTY
SQUARE

TELFAIR
SQUARE

W. PRESIDENT

WRIGHT
SQUARE

E PRESIDENT

OGLETHORPE
SQUARE

COLUMBIA
SQUARE

GREENE
SQUARE

W. YORK

E. YORK

W. OGLETHORPE

E. OGLETHORPE

W.HULL

E HULL

ORLEANS
SQUARE

W. MCDONOUGH

CHIPPEWA
SQUARE

E.MCDONOUGH

CLOLONIAL
PARK
CEMETERY

CRAWFORD
SQUARE

W. PERRY

E. PERRY

W. LIBERTY

E LIBERTY

E. LIBERTY

W. HARRIS

E. HARRIS

PALASKI
SQUARE

MADISON
SQUARE

LAFAYETTE
SQUARE

TROUP
SQUARE

W. CHARLTON

E. CHARLTON

W. JONES

E.JONES

W. TAYLOR

E. TAYLOR

CHATTAM
SQUARE

W. WAYNE

MONTERY
SQUARE

E. WAYNE

CALHOUN
SQUARE

WHITEFIELD
SQUARE

W. GORDON

E.GORDON

W. GASTON

E GASTON

W. HUNINGTON

E HUNINGTON

HALL

HALL

HALL

1. PINK HOUSE
2 TONY ROMAS
3 U.S. CUSTOM HOUSE
4 CITY HALL
5 INTERSECTION RIVER & MLK
6 FIRST AFRICAN BAPTIST CHURCH
7.JOHNSON SQUARE
8.WRIGHT SQUARE
9 JULIETTE GORDON LOW B.P.
10 INDEPENDANT PRESBYTERIAN
11.SAVANNAH THEATER
12 SORREL -WEED HOUSE

13 GREEN-MELDRIN HOUSE
14 BARTOW HOUSE
15 MOMTEREY SQUARE
16 OGLETHORPE SOCIAL CLUB
17 LAWTON HOUSE
18 FORSYTHE PARK

1 FORSYTHE PARK
2 CAHNDLER OAK
3.CALHOUN SQUARE
4.ANDREW LOW HOUSE
5.DEATH OF PHEOBE PEMBER
6 PORTER ALEXANDER HOUSE
7.SAINT VINCENTS ACADEMY
8 JOSEPH JOHNSTON HOUSE
9 COLONIAL CEMETERY
10 POLICE BARRACKS
11 PRESIDENTS INN
12 2ND AFRICAN BAPTIST CHURCH

13.EMMET PARK
14.MARSHAL HOUSE

6

The Savannah River from the Talmedge Bridge.

Chapter 1

Savannah Early in the War Tour

(You are standing in the middle of Reynolds' Square, our starting point. You should be standing in front of the John Wesley monument. From here we will move toward the Pink House Restaurant on your left.)

STOP 1:

The Pink House Restaurant, 23 Abercorn Street

The house was built in 1789 for James Habersham, Jr. From 1812 to 1861, it served as a branch of the Bank of the United States. During the Civil War, a bank operated here at this structure. When General Sherman's army moved into South Carolina, the acting provost marshal used the building as his headquarters during the occupation of Savannah. Lt. Colonel Robert York had been assigned as the provost marshal in January 1865; he had held the same position in Vicksburg after its surrender in July 1863.

(From here we are going to walk north one block to the intersection of Abercorn and East Bay Streets, the traffic light will indicate the direction of our move. Once on East Bay Street, turn left.)

The street that you are on now was and is one of Savannah's busiest economic arteries; it runs parallel to the Savannah River. It would be common to see carriages and wagons moving east and west along the street, as well as the cotton factors or traders, from the Cotton Exchange conducting business at nearby banks.

The Pink House was the headquarters for the Union
provost marshal during the occupation of Savannah.

STOP 2:

Tony Romas Restaurant, 7 East Bay Street

"in a few hours this city, in which I found a lawless mob of low whites and Negroes pillaging and setting fire to property, was reduced to order."[1]

General John Geary after taking possession
of Savannah

Until December 1864, this building served as the Bank of the Central Georgia Railroad. Major General John Geary had to send patrols through the city to quash the looting.[2] During Sherman's occupation of Savannah, General Geary established his headquarters here; it is comparatively close to the City Exchange, present day City Hall. Geary worked with Mayor Richard Arnold and his city council to keep order in the city, and he had accepted Arnold's surrender of the city. Geary was appointed to administer the occupation of Savannah because he had been the territorial governor of Kansas and the first mayor of San Francisco.[3]

Geary would later regain his command when Sherman's army marched into South Carolina.

(Continue to move west towards the intersection of Bull and Bay Streets.)

Tony Romas in December 1864 was Union
General John Geary's headquarters.

STOP 3:

United States' Customs House, 1 East Bay Street

The Customs House was designed by noted architect John Norris and was completed in 1852. It served as a post office, Federal Court, and as a Custom House before the war. The *Wanderer* Trial was conducted here in November 1859 and in May 1860; the US District Attorney, Henry Rootes Jackson, tried four Savannah businessmen for illegally trading slaves from West Africa. They were found not guilty because of insufficient evidence, but there were fines and some jail time.

Georgia seized the building after she seceded from the Union. The Confederate Stars and Bars were raised over the building in April 1861 by the Oglethorpe Light Infantry.

Sherman's troops paraded by the building after the surrender of the city in December 1864. It was placed on the National Register of Historic Places in 1974.

On weekdays, visitors are welcome to climb the steps and walk into the lobby.

(Cross Bay Street at the crosswalk and stand in front of the building with the gold dome.)

The United States Custom House was seized by
Georgia troops in January 1861.

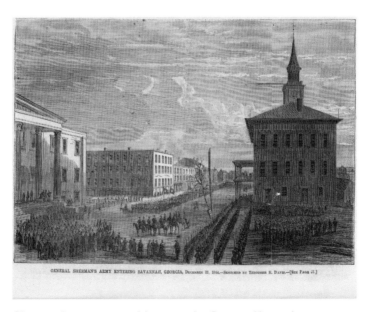

GENERAL SHERMAN'S ARMY ENTERING SAVANNAH, GEORGIA, December 21, 1864.—Sketched by Theodore R. Davis.—[See Page 51.]

Sherman's troops marching past the Custom House in
December 1864. *Courtesy of the Coastal Heritage
Society and Fort Jackson.*

STOP 4:

City Hall, intersection of Bull and Bay Streets

The present building was constructed in 1904, but it was formerly the City Exchange during the Civil War. Many town meetings were conducted here, such as the discussion about sending troops to Bleeding Kansas in 1856. Recruiters used the building to seek volunteers for the all Georgia Irish Brigade in 1861. Brigadier General Francis S. Bartow's body lay in state here for two days in late July 1861.

Edward C. Anderson, a plantation owner and a former officer in the United States Navy, was given the commission of a major in the Confederate army and was ordered by President Jefferson Davis to buy war material for the Confederacy and investigate the conduct of other Confederate agents in London.[4] He found that the funds he needed were insufficient and that Union agents were stalking him. Help arrived from Savannah, in the form of two cotton traders, Charles Green and Andrew Low.[5]

Anderson returned to Savannah in November 1861 and commanded all the coastal batteries until January 1865, when he was named the commandant of Charleston. He was elected mayor of Savannah in December 1865. Anderson died in 1883 and is buried in Laurel Grove Cemetery.[6]

(Turn right and walk along the north side of East Bay Street to the Abercorn Street Ramp, look to your left while walking.)

The bell on your right is the original bell that hung over the City Exchange until 1903. The bell rang each trade day, announcing the start and the end of the day's business along Factor's Walk. The bell was also used to announce important election and war news.

The Cotton Exchange bell is the only item left from
the old City Exchange building.

The pedestrian bridges on your left and ahead of you were constructed to allow the cotton factors an easier access to Bay Street and beyond.

(Proceed down the Abercorn Street ramp, moving towards its intersection with River Street.)

The building that comes into your front view was built in 1796 as part of the Savannah Cotton Exchange; the lower level was used for the storage of cotton. Cotton was stored in 500 lbs. bales. The second and third floors were where the factors, cotton traders, had their offices and conducted business. By 1860, Savannah set the price for cotton – a product so integral to the economy it was referred to as "white gold" – throughout the South.

Today the upper level is a bar, the Bayou Café, and the lower level is a restaurant that has been open since 1970.

(Turn left onto River Street; you are walking in a westerly direction.)

The buildings on your left were all rebuilt between 1885-1886. After the war started in 1861, cotton was stored here as part of the Cotton Embargo placed by Richmond to force the European powers to break the blockade and force an armistice between the North and the South.

As you walk down River Street, you will see a sign for Vic's on the River Restaurant & Bar; please go to the fourth floor. The restaurant welcomes visitors to view a map that was unearthed in 1901. It was drawn by officers from Sherman's army after the capture of Savannah. This building was used to quarter these soldiers during the occupation.

Walking west with the wharfs on your right, where the plaza is now, there would have been many steamers trading back and forth between Savannah and New York City until 1861. During the war, this area was used to build or refurbish ships for the Savannah River Squadron. The first iron clad in Savannah was the CSS *Atlanta,* launched in May 1862.

The island in the middle of the river is Hutchinson Island; a Confederate gun battery was placed on the eastern end to strengthen the Savannah River defenses.

The movie producers for *Glory* used River Street to depict Boston when the 54th Massachusetts marched off to war in 1863.

A present view of the cotton
warehouses along Factor's Walk.

*(Follow River Street, west-
ward, until it intersects with
Martin Luther King Boulevard.
In the 1860s, Martin Luther
King Boulevard was West
Broad Street. You will know
that you have reached the intersection when you see a
power plant on your right).*

STOP 5:

Intersection of River Street and Martin Luther King Boulevard

"take possession of Fort Pulaski and hold it against all persons to be abandoned only under orders from me or under compulsion by an overpowering hostile force."[7]

Georgia Governor Joseph Brown's orders to General Alexander Lawton

From this site on January 3, 1861, General Alexander Lawton of the Army of Georgia disembarked on the steamer *Ida* with the 1st Regiment and a battery of artillery. The force numbered close to 150 men. Their mission was to capture Fort Pulaski for the state of Georgia. From a balcony overlooking West Broad Street, Lawton cheered his troops as they marched in the rain to the wharf. The street was also lined with enthusiastic citizens.[8]

On the night of December 20, 1864, General William Hardee's 10,000 Confederate soldiers evacuated Savannah from this location. A crude pontoon bridge was constructed of rice boats, seventy-five and eighty feet in length. They were lashed end to end, instead of side to side, because of the lack of them and were anchored with railroad wheels. Many of the surrounding wharfs were torn up to provide planks for the bridge.[9] The bridge spanned from this point in front of you to Hutchinson Island, then crossed to Pennyworth Island and finally into the safety of South Carolina.[10]

(Turn left on Martin Luther King Boulevard.)

18

REMOVING THE OBSTRUCTIONS IN THE SOUTH CHANNEL OF THE SAVANNAH RIVER, GA., BELOW FORT JACKSON.

Confederate troops evacuating Savannah. *Courtesy of the Coastal Heritage Society and Fort Jackson.*

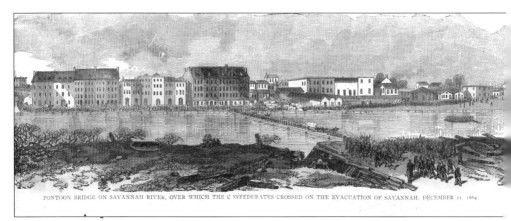

PONTOON BRIDGE ON SAVANNAH RIVER, OVER WHICH THE CONFEDERATES CROSSED ON THE EVACUATION OF SAVANNAH. DECEMBER 21, 1864.

Another view of the Confederate evacuation of Savannah. *Courtesy of the Coastal Heritage Society and Fort Jackson.*

This was a main artery that used to move people and cargo back and forth from the river.

(Follow Martin Luther King Boulevard until it intersects with Bryan Street and take a left, you are now heading east.)

You are now walking into the western end of City Market. On the left was a slave market. There are future plans to restore this building into a museum of the African-American slave experience in Savannah.

A present view of where Lawton's troops embarked for Fort
Pulaski and the Confederate evacuation in December 1864.

STOP 6:

First African
Baptist Church,
23 Montgomery Street

The church was built from 1855 to 1859. Slaves and freedmen generated all the money and labor. The lower level was used as a station for the Underground Railroad.

Escaped slaves made their way up the Savannah River towards Augusta and were helped by other conductors to make their way north, most likely to Canada.

The church is open for tours.
912-233-6597
Monday – Friday, 10:00 a.m. - 4:00 p.m.

(Please follow Bryan Street until it intersects with Bull Street at Johnson Square.)

As you walk into Johnson Square, look for the sundial on the southern end of the square. Stand here with your back to the sundial.

The First African Baptist Church has been
holding religious services since 1859.

STOP 7:

Johnson Square, intersection of Bryan and Bull Streets

"Brass bands were playing, rockets soaring, bonfires blazing; in fact the old town seemed to have gone crazy."[11]

Charles Olmstead, future Confederate colonel, on the anti-Lincoln Rally, November 8, 1860

This square was the first planned square, established in 1733, and became a focal point for Savannah's finances and, to some extent, a communication line to the outside world.

The monument in the center was dedicated to Revolutionary War General Nathaniel Greene, built between 1825 and 1830.

On the evening of November 8, 1860, a crowd estimated to be about 3,000 persons occupied the entire square and surrounding streets. They gathered about this monument to protest the election of Abraham Lincoln. Lincoln's name did not appear on the ballots in Savannah or Georgia.

Savannahians and all Southerners were trying to invoke the Revolutionary ghosts that won America's independence from Great Britain. They were calling this event the Second American Revolution.

Pulaski Hotel, present day Regents Bank, 1 West Bryan Street

"I concluded I had had enough of the President and so put about, and making a safe escape from the crowd. I would up the evening by calling on a pretty sweetheart of mine here, which was far more to my taste I assure you that to from one of the crowd who with open mouths and strained eyeballs, gape after the coattails of the President."[12]

A bored Savannah citizen listening to Jefferson Davis' speech, October 1863

24

The Greene Monument was the center-
piece for political rallies in late 1860.

There was plenty of excitement and prejudice as the crowd focused its attention on the Pulaski Hotel on November 8, 1860. Speakers used the second floor balcony as a platform to deliver anti-Lincoln speeches and preach about Northern injustices against the South. The rally turned into a party rather than a protest, in less than one year's time Savannah was poised to be invaded.

A crowd gathered again, six weeks later, on December 26, 1860, to show support for South Carolina's secession. They had been asked to illuminate their homes to show support for Georgia's secession from the Union. Some of the crowd had brought torches to further display their support for solidarity with South Carolina, challenging Georgia to follow South Carolina. People in the square were wearing secession cockades made of Palmetto leaves.[13] Again, secessionist speakers used the Pulaski Hotel to deliver their fiery rhetoric.

During the war, Governor Brown made speeches here to help rally support for the war.

Generals Robert E. Lee and Pierre G. T. Beauregard, as commanders of the Department of South Carolina, Georgia, and East Florida held staff meetings at the hotel when he visited Savannah between 1862 and 1864.

Jefferson Davis made a speech here on the portico in October 1863, after inspecting the Savannah River fortifications.[14]

Between 1865-67, Varina Davis, wife of Jefferson Davis, and her two children were placed under house arrest in the confines of the hotel while her husband had quarters courtesy of the United States at Fortress Monroe.

(Turn right and walk towards the southeast corner of the square.)

Christ Church, 28 Bull Street

"Pray for Jeff Davis, why certainly. You ought to pray for him everyday, for Jeff Davis needs praying very much."[15]

General Sherman, when asked by the Reverend if it would be proper to pray for the Confederate president, December 1864

26

Built in 1838, it continued to serve as a house of worship during the war years.

On July 28, 1861, a funeral service was held here to honor one of Savannah's most prominent citizens, Francis S. Bartow. Bartow was a Confederate brigadier general who fell at the Battle of First Manassas on July 21, 1861. His funeral procession went down Whitaker Street.

In late October 1863, President Jefferson Davis attended services here while stopping at Savannah during his Southern states tour after the Battle of Chickamauga.

General Sherman and his staff attended services here after the surrender of the city.

Fire damaged the church in 1898; it was rebuilt with the original walls intact.

(Turn around and head towards Bull Street in a southerly direction, the gold dome of city hall should be behind you.)

You are now walking on one of the oldest streets in Savannah. In May 1861, Captain Francis S. Bartow marched up the street with the Oglethorpe Light Infantry as they were ordered to Winchester, Virginia.

(Continue down Bull Street until you reach Wright Square, stand to the left of the monument that sits in the center of the square.)

The Christ Church held General Francis S. Bartow's funeral in July 1861, saw President Jefferson Davis in attendance in October 1863, and General William Sherman during the occupation.

STOP 8:

William Washington Gordon Monument, center of Wright Square

The monument was erected by the city in 1883 to honor the founder of the Central of Georgia Railroad; the line was constructed in the early 1840s, allowing the port of Savannah to become the dominant city for setting cotton prices. There had been a competition between Georgia and South Carolina for the quick establishment of a cotton transportation network into their respective state's interiors. Georgia won.

(Keep moving south on the left side of the square, along the east side of Bull Street to the intersection with Oglethorpe Avenue and stop at the corner.)

If you look up at the relief on the monument, you can see the artist's rendition of the importance of Savannah's cotton trade, linking Savannah with Macon and western South Carolina. Reading the relief from right to left, you can visualize the train transporting cotton from the fields to the awaiting ships along the Savannah River.

The relief on the William Gordon Monument shows the
importance to the Central of Georgia Railroad to
Savannah's cotton economy.

STOP 9:

Juliette Gordon Low Birthplace, intersection of Bull Street and Oglethorpe Avenue,10 East Oglethorpe Avenue

"I shouldn't wonder if my papa did it! He has shot lots of Yankees."[16]

Four-year-old Juliette Gordon commenting on General Howard's amputated arm from the Battle of Fair Oaks, December 1864

This home was built in 1821 for James Moore Wayne, the mayor of Savannah at that time and it was sold to William Washington Gordon in 1831. Juliette Gordon Low, founder of the Girl Scouts of America, was born here on Halloween night in 1860. She and her mother had an audience with Generals Sherman and Howard when she was a precocious four year old in December 1864.

Her father was a supply officer for General Joe Wheeler's Confederate cavalry and later became a general of volunteers during the Spanish-American War. The mansion was marked as a National Historic Landmark in 1965. The Girl Scouts of America own and operate the museum.

The house is now a museum and is open for tours. The museum interprets the Civil War years every Monday. 912-233-4501 www.girlscouts.org/birthplace Monday - Saturday, 10:00 a.m. - 4:00 p.m. Sunday, 12:30 pm - 4:30 p.m. Closed on Wednesdays.

(Cross Oglethorpe Avenue and stop in front of the Chatham County Board of Education, facing the church. The best view is here.)

Julliette Gordon Low and her mother entertained
General Sherman here in December 1864.

STOP 10:

Independent Presbyterian Church, 207 Bull Street

"All young, all unmarried, all gentlemen, there was not one of the killed, who was not an ornament to his community and freighted with brilliant promise."[17]

Savannah *Daily Morning News*
on Savannahians that fell at
First Manassas, February 1862

The church was originally built in 1818, but was rebuilt after a devastating fire in 1889.

In February 1862, nine Savannahians killed at the Battle of First Manassas had their funeral services here before being laid to rest at the Laurel Grove Cemetery. These soldiers had been temporarily interred on the Virginia battlefield.

The steeple of the church is famous for the opening credits from *Forrest Gump*.
912-236-3346
The church is open on Friday afternoons.

(Continue moving south on Bull Street into the next square, Chippewa. Upon entering the square, walk over to the left in front of the Savannah Theater.)

A funeral was held at the Independent Presbyterian
Church in February 1862 for nine Savannahians who
were killed at the Battle of First Manassas.

STOP 11:

Savannah Theater, 222 Bull Street

"The General entered the house accompanied by but a single friend, the audience at once rose and spontaneously greeted the veteran with cheer after cheer."[18]

Daily Herald reporting on General Sherman's visit in May 1865

The original theater was built in 1818; this site has been active as a theater since its construction. Fires over the years have forced reconstruction.

Assassin John Wilkes Booth and his brother performed here in the late 1850s.

General Sherman was part of the audience of the theater in May 1865 as he was in Savannah to help oversee the dispensing of food and clothing to the local population.[19]

It is America's oldest running theater. The lobby doors are open during the day and the theater welcomes visitors to explore its history.

(Continue down Bull Street to Madison Square.)

As you come upon the intersection of Bull and Liberty Streets, look over to the Hilton Hotel on your left. On this site stood the Oglethorpe Barracks, a United States army post until 1861. The barracks managed and maintained both Forts Jackson and Pulaski. In early 1861, Captain William Whitting commanded the post; later he would become a Confederate general. Whitting was not present in the city when Lawton seized Fort Pulaski; it probably would not have mattered, for Whitting was from Mississippi. The barracks were seized on February 1861. Until December 1864, the barracks served as a headquarters and a hospital.[20]

During the war, the barracks were converted into a hospital.

(Stop at the pumpkin colored house on your right.)

The Savannah Theater saw a performance by
John Wilkes Booth in the late 1850s.

STOP 12:

Sorrel – Weed House, 6 West Harris Street

"For my part, when the time comes to cross the river like the others, I shall be found asking at the gates above, where is the Army of Northern Virginia? For there I will make my camp."[21]

General G. Moxley Sorrel

This house was constructed in 1841 and was the boyhood home of one of the youngest Confederate generals, G. Moxley Sorrel. Sorrel was born in 1838.

Sorrel served as Lt. General James Longstreet's Chief of Staff from July 1861 to May 1864. In May 1864, Sorrel led a counterattack against the Army of the Potomac's Second Corps along the Brock Road during the Battle of the Wilderness. The attack almost split the Union Army in two, but Longstreet and some of his staff were raked by friendly fire, forcing Lee to pause and reorganize.

In October 1864, Sorrel was promoted to a brigadier general at the age of twenty-six. He commanded a Georgia brigade in Lt. General A. P. Hill's Third Corps until he was wounded at Hatcher's Run, near Petersburg, Virginia, in February 1865.

After the war, Sorrel rejoined the banking industry, served on city council, and became the president of the Ocean Steamship Company. Sorrel also penned his experiences of the war, *Recollections of a Confederate Staff Officer*, recently re-titled *At the Right Hand of Longstreet*. Sorrel died in 1901 and is buried in Laurel Grove Cemetery.
912-925-3002
www.savannahtours.com
Open everyday, 10:00 am to 5:00 p.m.

l

(Continue south on Bull Street to the Green-Meldrim House on your right.)

The Sorrel-Weed House was the boyhood home of one
of the youngest Confederate generals, G. Moxley Sorrel.

STOP 13:

Green-Meldrim House, 14 Macon Street

"To His Excellency, President Lincoln,
Dear Sir,
I beg to present you as a Christmas Gift, the City of Savannah with 150 heavy guns and plenty of ammunition; and also about 25,000 bales of cotton."[22]

Major General William T. Sherman

The house was built in 1853. It was the home of Charles Green, a successful cotton factor. Green had arrived from Great Britain in the early 1830s and worked with Andrew Low, another successful factor.

Green traveled to Great Britain in July 1861, with money from both the Confederate government and the state of Georgia, to buy weapons. He helped ship arms and ammunition for the Southern war effort.[23] He was dispatched by the Confederate Secretary of War to try and push stalled efforts.[24] Major Edward Anderson had been having trouble negotiating with the English for loans.

Upon his return Green also tried to help the Confederacy by smuggling medicine into the South, but United States' authorities arrested him in Detroit while he was crossing in from Canada. He and his sister were placed in prison at Fort Warren in Boston Harbor. Eliza Low was released after eight days when she promised not to enter the "states under insurrection" without secretary of State Seward's permission.[25] British diplomats secured Green's freedom and safe passage back to Savannah in March 1862.

Green continued to support the Confederate war effort until December 1864 when Union troops occupied Savannah. In an effort to avoid any destruction or theft of the house, Green offered it for use to Union forces. It became General William T. Sherman's headquarters from December 1864 to January 1865. Sherman sent the message giving President Lincoln the

The Green-Meldrim House was built in 1853 and served as General Sherman's headquarters for eight weeks.

city of Savannah as a Christmas gift from this house. Sherman celebrated both Christmas and New Year's here. On December 26, Sherman issued Special Order No. 143, stating that Savannah and the surrounding country was held as a military outpost and was adopted for future military use.[26]

The house was sold after Green's death in 1881 to Judge Peter Meldrim and then to St. John's Church in 1943. The house now serves as a parish house and has been restored with furniture from the Civil War period. The house is open for tours.
912-233-3845
Tuesday,Thursday,and Saturday, 10:00 a.m. to 4:00 p.m.

St. John's Church

The existing church was built between 1852-53. The women of the church established a hospital in January 1862.[27] The church was known for it's chimes, but the chimes annoyed General Sherman during the occupation. According to popular folklore, Sherman ordered the bells dismantled, shipped North, and recast as Yankee cannon.

There are two different accounts for how the chimes were saved. In one, Joseph Fay, the donor of the chimes, appealed directly to Sherman to save the bells. In the other account, Fay called on President Lincoln to intervene.

(Walk past the front entrance, crossing Whitaker and Barnard Streets to Pulaski Square. As you enter the square, turn right and stand in front of the yellow house on the corner of West Harris and Barnard Streets.)

General Sherman threatened to recast the bells of St John's Church into artillery cannons because he thought them too annoying.

STOP 14:

Francis S. Bartow House, 126 West Harris Street

"They have killed me, boys, but never give up the field."

**Brigadier General Francis Bartow
at First Manassas**

The house was constructed in 1839. Francis S. Bartow was born in Savannah in 1819. Bartow became a prominent attorney and prestigious speaker in Savannah during the 1850s. In 1858, he ran for a Georgia congressional seat, but lost. With the ongoing unrest, Bartow put in much time with the Oglethorpe Light Infantry, a Savannah militia unit.

In the militia, Bartow held the rank of captain and was part of the Georgia expedition that seized Fort Pulaski on January 3, 1861.

Two weeks later he was representing Savannah at Georgia's Secession Convention, which met at Milledgeville on January 19. After Georgia seceded, Bartow represented Georgia at the Provisional Confederate Congress in Montgomery, Alabama, where they were organizing a government and electing leaders.

Bartow was a leader in the organization of the Confederate armies and chose the color of its uniforms, gray. He looked favorably at the uniforms of the Savannah Volunteer Guards, another local militia unit.

After the firing on Fort Sumter, Bartow learned that he had been elected to the Confederate Congress, but turned it down, choosing instead to serve the military. Bartow offered Company B of the Oglethorpe Light Infantry to Confederate service; it was quickly accepted. Bartow and his unit were mustered into the 8th Georgia Infantry at Winchester, Virginia, in June 1861. He was given command of the Eighth with the rank of colonel.

By July, Bartow was promoted to a brigadier general and commanded a brigade that served in the Shenandoah Valley until they were ordered to Manassas.

This was the home of General Francis S. Bartow, one
of Savannah's first casualties of the Civil War.

Bartow, Evans, and Bee's Brigades held positions on Matthews Hill on July 21, 1861, until a Federal flank attack took Bartow's life while he tried to rally his men. There is a marker on the battlefield indicating where he fell. He is buried at Laurel Grove Cemetery.

(After you have finished, turn back around and walk south on Barnard Street. Continue on Barnard until it intersects with Jones Street. Turn left on Jones.)

You are now walking east on Jones Street; many of these elaborate town houses on both sides of the street were built between 1845 and 1861, so this area was a very popular residential section of Savannah during the war.

(Continue down Jones until it intersects with Bull Street, make a right and walk until you reach Monterey Square.)

Bust of Francis Bartow in Forsyth Park.

Jones Street – many of the townhouses along this
street were constructed before the Civil War.

STOP 15:

Monterey Square, intersection of Bull and Taylor Streets

Monterey Square was one of the last squares constructed in Savannah. The Pulaski Monument was placed in the center of the square in 1854.

Hugh Comer House, 2 East Taylor Street

The Brown house on the corner of Bull and East Taylor Streets was constructed in 1880. In 1886, former Confederate President Jefferson Davis was a guest of Comer during the centennial celebration of the Chatham Artillery. Davis used the front porch as a platform to speak to Savannahians who gathered around the house to pay respects to him.

(Turn back around and walk past the monument, turn right. Stand in front of the red brick mansion, Mercer House.)

Mercer House, 429 Bull Street

"Eight years ago I shot a man who was standing right about where you are now. In a few weeks I'll be going on trial for murder, for the fourth time, and my lawyer is a man of expensive tastes. Make it twenty-five thousand and you have a deal."[28]

Jim Williams, while negotiating a contract with the producers of *Glory* to use his house in their film

Architect John Norris was hired by a United States' army colonel, Hugh Mercer, in 1860 to build this house. The outbreak of war delayed its completion until after the war.

Hugh Mercer was born at Fredericksburg, Virginia, in 1808 and was a graduate of West Point. The career army man married a woman from Savannah and made this city his home.

When war broke out, Mercer commanded a brigade in the Department of South Carolina, Georgia, and East Florida. Mercer had designed most of the fortifications east of the city between 1862 and 1863.

REVIEW OF CONFEDERATE TROOPS EN ROUTE TO VIRGINIA, AS THEY PASS THE PULASKI MONUMENT, SAVANNAH, GA., AUGUST 7TH, 1861.

The Oglethorpe Light Infantry marching around Monterey Square while leaving Savannah for Virginia in May 1861. *Courtesy of the Coastal Heritage Society and Fort Jackson.*

A present view of Monterey Square.

In 1864, Mercer and his brigade were transferred to the Army of the Tennessee for the defense of Atlanta. By July, after some hard campaigning, he became sickly and was forced to resign his command.

Mercer returned to Savannah in an effort to restore his health. Once healthy, Mercer and his son helped erect some fortifications west of the city. He helped defend the city during the siege and evacuated into South Carolina on December 20. Mercer would later surrender with the Army of Tennessee in North Carolina in April 1865.

After the war, Mercer was employed as a banker in Baltimore and would die while visiting Germany in 1877. His grandson was Johnny Mercer, the famed songwriter.

In 1988, the owner of Mercer House, Jim Williams, was on his fourth trial for murder, as written in *Midnight in the Garden of Good and Evil.* He was short on funds to pay his legal team, so the producers of *Glory* offered Williams $25,000 to use his house in the film. It was shown early in the film when Robert Gould Shaw, played by Matthew Broderick, was offered command of the 54th Massachusetts Infantry Regiment.

In the mid-1970s, another film company was in the area filming *The Lincoln Conspiracy.* They chose the homes around Monterey Square to set as downtown Washington, D.C. during the Civil War. Williams, tired of the inconvenience and the possibility of the exterior of his house being filmed, hung a swastika at the front of the house in an effort to deter the filmmakers.

The house is open for tours.
912-236-6352
www.mercerhouse.com
Monday – Saturday, 10:30 a.m. - 3:30 p.m.
Sunday, 12:30 pm - 4:30 p.m.
Closed on Wednesdays and most holidays.

(Turn around and head back to the center of the square, turn right onto the left side of Bull Street, stopping at the Oglethorpe Social Club.)

The Hugh Comer House had former Confederate
President Jefferson Davis as a guest in 1886.

The Mercer House was started in 1860, but the war
interrupted its completion until 1868.

STOP 16:

Oglethorpe Social Club, 450 Bull Street

"Whether the General [Howard] relented, or whether I myself was to blame, I don't know; yet both the liquors and the books, together with other articles, found their way into our Headquarters," confessed Captain Bedford. "We had no respect for the English Government and none for its flag."[29]

Captain Bedford, United States Army

This home was constructed in 1857 for Edmund Molyneux, the British Consul for Savannah during the Civil War. Molyneux helped secure loans through his friends to help buy arms and ammunition for the Confederacy.[30]

Molyneux owned some cotton when Sherman arrived, but it was quickly seized by Federal authorities. He asked Sherman for the return of the cotton because he was a British subject, but Sherman replied that the British would be treated like Americans who "openly smuggle arms to kill us."[31]

During the Union occupation of Savannah, Major General Oliver O. Howard who commanded the right wing of Sherman's March, used this house as his headquarters. During the army's occupation of the house they took advantage of the wine, brandy, and books that were owned by Molyneux. Molyneux later filed an $11,000 lawsuit against the United States, but it was simply ignored.[32]

This house was later the home of former Confederate Brigadier General Henry Rootes Jackson. Jackson was born in Savannah in 1820. Before the Civil War he was an attorney and a veteran of the Mexican War. During the Mexican War, he raised and commanded the Irish Jasper Greens, another local militia unit.

After the Mexican War, Jackson served as a federal prosecutor until the mid-1850s, when he became the ambassador to Austria.

In 1859, he was assigned as the special prosecutor in the *Wanderer* Trial. He failed to convict the four Savannahians that were on trial for illegally importing slaves. Jackson also represented Savannah at Georgia's secession convention.

When the Civil War erupted, Jackson was appointed a judge of the Confederate courts in Georgia, but resigned to accept a commission as a brigadier general. Governor Brown asked Jackson to command a division of Georgia state troops for six months, he accepted, but it was against the wishes of President Davis. The Confederate conscription act of 1862 left Jackson without a command. From April 1862 to the start of the Atlanta Campaign in 1864, he served as an aid to General W. H. Walker.

Jackson commanded a brigade of Georgia troops from the Atlanta Campaign to the Battle of Nashville. On December 16, Jackson was captured, along with his entire brigade, when overrun by Union forces. He spent some time on the Johnson Island Prison Camp, along Ohio's Lake Erie shore and was later moved to Fort Warren.

After the war, he continued to practice law and served as Minister to Mexico between 1885-86. Jackson died in 1898 and is buried at Bonaventure Cemetery.

(Cross Bull Street at Gaston Street, walking west along the north side of Gaston Street. Stop at 20 West Gaston Street.)

The Oglethorpe Social Club was a home built for British Consul Edward Moleneux in 1857.

STOP 17:

Alexander Lawton House, 20 West Gaston Street

This antebellum house was occupied by Alexander Lawton during the years preceding the Civil War. Lawton was born in nearby Beaufort, South Carolina, in 1818 and he graduated West Point in 1839. He served with the United States' army during the war with Mexico. After the Mexican War, he was a practicing attorney in Savannah and Governor Joseph Brown named him commander of the Army of Georgia in 1860.

Lawton led Georgia's seizure of Fort Pulaski in January 1861. After the Union capture of Fort Pulaski in April 1862, Lawton was ordered, with 5,000 troops from the Savannah area, to the Confederate army gathering around Richmond. That army would later become the Army of Northern Virginia. He commanded a brigade of Georgia troops from the Peninsula Campaign to Sharpsburg. At Sharpsburg, Lawton was seriously wounded and did not return to service until August 1863, and then served as the Quartermaster of the Confederacy until the end of the war.

After the war, Lawton returned to Savannah to practice law and served as Minister to Austria in 1886 and died at Clifton Springs, New York, in 1887. He is buried at Laurel Grove Cemetery.

(Cross Gaston Street into Forsyth Park.)

Confederate General Alexander Lawton lived
here, before the Civil War began, as an attorney.

STOP 18:

Forsyth Park

The park today covers twenty acres and was named for Governor John Forsyth. It was laid out in 1851. Confederate troops drilled here in 1861 and 1862. On the last Sunday in April, Confederate Memorial Day is celebrated in the center of the park. Other festivities occur throughout the year.

Fountain
The fountain was placed in 1858 and was restored in 1988.

The Fountain was placed in the park in 1858.

Confederate Monument

The monument was erected between 1874 and 1875; you are standing in an area that was utilized by the local militia before hostilities broke out. It is made of Canadian sandstone and the buttons on his frock coat represent all the Confederate States. The busts of Generals Francis S. Bartow and Lafayette McLaws guard the perimeter of the monument.

Confederate re-enactors celebrate Confederate Memorial Day on the last Sunday of each April.

Chapter 2
Savannah Late in the War and After Tour

STOP 1:
Confederate Monument

The monument in Forsyth Park was erected between 1874 and 1875; you are standing in an area that was utilized by the local militia before hostilities broke out. It is made of Canadian sandstone and the buttons on his frock coat represent all the Confederate States. The busts of Generals Francis S. Bartow and Lafayette McLaws guard the perimeter of the monument.

(Standing in front of the monument, walk to the left to Drayton Street, cross the street – Huntingdon – and walk north along Drayton until to you come to the vacant hospital on your right. Move over to the large Live Oak tree inside the fencing. Stop here.)

A stockade was built around this oak tree in 1864 to secure Union prisoners of war.

STOP 2:

Warren A. Chandler Hospital

The hospital was founded in 1803 for the poor and local seamen. It was incorporated in 1808 as the Savannah Poor House and Hospitality Society. The current hospital in front of you was built in 1819.

During the war, the hospital was operated by civilians and a stockade was built around the Live Oak to confine Union prisoners of war. It became a hospital for Union soldiers from 1865 to 1866.

In 1872, the hospital became the Savannah Hospital. It was bought by the Methodist Church and was renamed Bishop Warren A. Chandler Hospital in honor of the bishop himself. The site is presently vacant, as the new hospital was constructed south of here.

(Continue north on Drayton and turn right onto East Gaston Street. Walk along Gaston Street until it intersects with Abercorn Street and turn left. You are now moving north towards Calhoun Square.)

STOP 3:

Calhoun Square

This square was named after the famed South Carolina politician John C. Calhoun. The townhouses around this square were constructed after 1855, so you are in another residential section that is still pretty much intact from the Civil War era.

Massey School
The school served as Union hospital between 1864 and 1865.

(Continue down Abercorn until you reach the next square, Lafayette. Position yourself in front of the large mansion on your left. It is almost a whitewash pink color.)

The school served as a military hospital late in the war.

STOP 4:

Andrew Low House, 329 Abercorn Street

The house was built in 1849 for Andrew Low, a wealthy British cotton merchant. Robert E. Lee visited the home in 1861 and was guest here with his daughter in 1870.

Julliette Gordon Low founded the Girl Scouts of America here in 1912.

Andrew Low arrived with his wife in Great Britain in August 1861. He brought codes of signals to pass information between Richmond and London.[33] They later left for Canada with messages from Anderson on tissue paper that was hid in Mrs. Low's bonnet.[34]

Andrew Low and his wife returned to the United States, but were arrested in Cincinnati while en route to Savannah. Secretary of State William H. Seward, charging Low as a Confederate collaborator and agent in Great Britain, gave the arrest order. Low was confined to Fort Warren in Boston and his pregnant wife was detained in Washington.[35] Low's wife was later paroled to a home in Baltimore and sixty days later he was able join his pregnant wife. Both were released and allowed to return to Savannah in March 1862. Federal authorities had confused Andrew Low with his nephew John, who was in Great Britain helping the Confederate naval effort.[36]

Low's nephew, John, also the son-in-law to Charles Green, was involved early in the war in the Confederate naval effort in Savannah. He was appointed a lieutenant in the Confederate States Navy.[37] Low and Captain James D. Bulloch loaded the *Fingal* with cotton and resin so it could be traded in Great Britain for military supplies, but they were unable to penetrate the Union blockade.[38] John Low was forced to board a train for Wilmington, North Carolina; Low had given up on trying to get the *Fingal* out. Charles Green was already in Great Britain visiting.

Low also served on the famous Confederate raiders, the CSS *Alabama* and *Florida*.

The mansion is open for tours.
912-232-8200
Monday – Saturday, 10:30
a.m. - 4:00 p.m.
Sunday, 12:00 pm - 4:00 p.m.
Closed on Thursdays and national holidays.

*(Cross the street and stand in
front of the Lafayette.)*

The home of former cotton trader and Confederate agent Andrew Low.

STOP 5:

Phebe Yates Pember funeral, 321 Abercorn Street. The Lafayette

"No one slept during the night of horror, for added to present scenes were the anticipations of what morrow would bring forth. Daylight downed upon a wreck of destruction and desolation"[39]

Phoebe Yates Pember on the evacuation of Richmond, April 2, 1865

Phebe Yates was born in Charleston in August 1823 and moved to Savannah around 1853. She married Thomas Pember in early 1861, but he died a few months later of tuberculosis.[40]

In December 1862, Yates Pember was appointed chief matron of a division at Chimborozo Hospital in Richmond. This hospital was probably the finest military hospital of the entire war. She stayed behind with her patients after the evacuation of Richmond in April 1865.

Yates Pember returned briefly to Savannah after the war and then moved to Baltimore, where she penned her memoirs in 1879, *A Southern Woman's Story,* her account of the Confederate nursing experience.[41]

She died in 1913, a private funeral was held at this site, and she is buried in Laurel Grove Cemetery. On June 29, 1995, the United States Postal Service issued a series of stamps depicting events and people from the Civil War; Phebe Yates Pember was on one those stamps.[42]

(Turn left onto East Harris towards the corner. Cross the street at Pinky Masters, our stop is the house on the right.)

66

Former Confederate nurse Phoebe Yates Pember
died in a friend's house on this square in 1913.

STOP 6:

Edward Porter Alexander House, 104 East Harris Street

"Our men were good enough; the only trouble was that there were not enough of them."[43]

Colonel Edward P. Alexander on the failure of Pickett's Charge at Gettysburg

Brigadier General Edward Porter Alexander was born in Washington, Georgia, in 1835 and graduated West Point in 1857. He began the war as a signal officer, but was later transferred to the artillery. Alexander fought in all major campaigns of the Army of Northern Virginia, as Longstreet's I Corps artillery chief. After the war, he worked in the railroad industry and held some small public offices. While in Savannah during the 1880s and early 1890s, Alexander served as President of the Savannah and Memphis Railroad. He died in Savannah in 1910 while visiting family. He is buried in Augusta.

(Walk back into the square, and continue up Abercorn Street on the side closest to the Cathedral and turn right onto Liberty Street. St Vincent's is on your right.)

This was home of Confederate General Edward Porter Alexander after the Civil War when he served as president of the Savannah and Memphis Railroad.

69

STOP 7:

St. Vincent's

This school opened in 1845. The Sisters of Mercy cared for the wounded during the Civil War.

Jefferson Davis' children, Winnie and Jeff Davis, attended the school from 1865 to 1867 while they and their mother, Varina, were basically under house arrest during Jefferson Davis' incarceration at Fortress Moultrie. Today it is a private girls school.

(Continue walking up Abercorn Street, but cross on the other side of the street, to the intersection with East Oglethorpe Avenue, turn left and stop at 105 East Oglethorpe Avenue. There is a fire station at the corner where you make the left turn.)

STOP 8:

Joseph E. Johnston House, 105 East Oglethorpe Avenue

"If I were in his place, and he were standing in mine, he would not put on his hat."[44]

General Joseph E. Johnston at Sherman's funeral in March 1891

This home was built in 1821 and was the residence of former Confederate General Joseph E. Johnston from 1868 to 1876. Johnston helped establish the Palmer & Cay Insurance Company. Robert E. Lee visited Johnston here in April 1870. Johnston wrote his war memoirs here in 1874, *Narrative of Military*

Operations, Directed, During the Late War Between the States. After leaving Savannah, he served as U.S. representative from Virginia between 1879-1881 and was later appointed commissioner of railroads between 1885 and 1891. He would catch pneu-

(Retrace your steps back to Abercorn Street and enter the Colonial Cemetery. Move through by making a right towards the southwest corner of the cemetery).

Confederate General Joseph E. Johnston's residence after the war while in Savannah.

STOP 9:

Colonial Cemetery

The cemetery opened in 1750 and was closed in 1853 with over 10,000 people buried here. It is thought that the occupation of the cemetery by Sherman's troops caused much damage. Headstones had been altered and knocked over. After Sherman's troops left, some Savannahians came in to repair the damage. There was no strong documentation on where people were buried. Only 600 of those 10,000 were identified. The cemetery was reopened as a park in 1896.

(Go past the light post on the far right and look for a headstone just left of the post. It has a cross at the top and belongs to Maurice Cody.)

Maurice Cody Gravesite
Before 1864, Maurice Cody died at the age of 47; after 1865 he died at the age of 147.

(Follow the path in front of you to the brick wall on the east side of the cemetery, look at the headstones that are mounted here.)

This headstone was altered in December 1864 by Union troops that bivouacked in the cemetery.

The East Wall

The headstones that remained intact but could not be reunited with their owners were relocated to the back wall between 1865 and 1866.

(Exit out the gate on East Oglethorpe Avenue, cross the street onto Lincoln Street to President's Quarters. You will turn left on East York Street. The President's Quarters is on your right.)

Gravestones were placed on the wall by 1866, after citizens failed to match them to their owners.

STOP 10:

Savannah Police Barracks

The barracks were constructed between 1868 and 1869, after the reorganization of the Savannah police force in November 1859 by Robert H. Anderson. Anderson saw action at Fort McAlister in 1863 and later was a brigadier general with General Joe Wheeler's cavalry. He served as chief of police until February 1888, when he passed away. He is buried in Bonaventure Cemetery.[45]

The police force was strongly organized by General Anderson after the war; the barracks was constructed in 1869.

STOP 11:

President's Quarters Inn, 217 & 219 East York Street

These homes were built in 1855 as rental units, the house facing south was Alexander Lawton's home after the war. Robert E. Lee visited Lawton here in 1870. Crowds gathered around the house, making it difficult for Lee to rest, so he left with his daughter through a back exit to spend the rest of his stay at the home of Andrew Low.[46]

These homes were fully restored in 1986.

(Turn right onto Abercorn along the parking lot of the President's Quarters and then turn right onto East President Street and continue eastward until you intersect with Houston Street and turn left.)

Robert E. Lee stayed here as a guest of General
Alexander Lawton in 1870 before gathering crowds
forced him to relocate to the Andrew Low House.

STOP 12:

Bryan Baptist Church

"40 acres and a mule."

General William T. Sherman

Originally, this church was known as the Second African Baptist Church. It was organized here in 1802. In January 1865, Sherman issued Field Order #15, by which free slaves from all of the islands south of Charleston to the St. John's River in north Florida were to receive abandoned rice fields ranging from the ocean front up to thirty miles inland that had been set aside in a "40 acres and a mule" settlement.[47] Twenty black ministers joined Secretary of War Edwin M. Stanton and Sherman, meeting at this location before Sherman issued his order. Slaves freed in Savannah were allowed to remain in their chosen or accustomed vocations, but were subject to military authority; however, on the islands and settlements hereafter no white person would be allowed to live in these settlements and the management of the former slaves' affairs was to be left to them.[48] The church was rebuilt in 1925 after a fire.

(Continue north on Houston until it intersects with East Bay Street. Cross the street into Emmet Park.)

The Mulberry Inn was a cotton warehouse during the Civil War. You will pass this on your right.

(Turn left in Emmet Park and stop at the first monument on your right.)

80

The Second African Baptist Church
was rebuilt after a fire in 1926.

STOP 13:

Emett Park

Chatham Artillery Monument

This militia unit was founded in 1786. It participated in the capture of Fort Pulaski in January 1861. During the war, the artillery unit was assigned to the Department of South Carolina, Georgia, and East Florida, serving around the Savannah area at the following locations, Skidaway Island, Green Island, Coffee Bluff, and Fort Jackson. The unit also fought at Battery Wagner in July 1863 and Olustee, Florida, in February 1864. It finished out the war with the Army of Tennessee in April 1865. The monument was dedicated in 1986.

(Continue walking west through Emmet Park along East Bay Street and turn left onto Abercorn Street and turn right onto Broughton.)

The Chatham Artillery served from the Revolutionary War to the Second World War.

STOP 14:

Marshall House,
123 East Broughton Street

The hotel opened its doors to 135 guests in 1857. Renovations quickly followed and it was reopened in November 1859 after the completion of the iron veranda on the second floor.[49] The Stars and Bars was hoisted over the hotel early in the morning of March 6, 1861. It served as a hospital in the later war years.

The Marshall House closed in 1957, but was brought back to life through renovations that ended in 1999.

The Marshall House was built in 1855 and
was fully restored in 1999.

Chapter 3

Savannah's Eastern Defenses Driving Tour

(This tour will start at the Savannah Visitors Center and History Museum on Martin Luther King Jr. Boulevard. The parking lot is accessible from Oglethorpe Avenue.)

STOP 1:

Savannah Visitors Center and History Museum, 301 Martin Luther King Boulevard

The museum offers an exceptional history on naval operations around Savannah during the Civil War. There are models of two ironclads, the CSS *Savannah* and *Georgia*. Other displays include weapons and a Confederate frame torpedo.
912-651-6825
www.chsgeorgia.org/shm/home.htm
Monday – Friday, 8:30 a.m. - 5:00 p.m.
Saturday – Sunday, 9:00 a.m. - 5:00 p.m.
Closed Thanksgiving, Christmas, and New Years' Day.

(After exiting the parking lot, drive until you come to a light on Oglethorpe Avenue, turn right. Stay on Oglethorpe until the next light, where you make a left turn onto Martin Luther King Jr. Boulevard. Stay on Martin Luther King until it intersects with West Bay Street, .3 miles. Turn right onto West Bay Street. We are now driving east towards Fort Jackson.)

As Bay Street veers to the right, the Marriot Hotel will come into view on your left. Along the left side of this road was a Confederate battery called Bay Battery.

A bale of cotton on exhibit at the
Savannah History Museum.

Bay Battery

This battery consisted of one 32-pound gun.[50]

(Turn left onto President Street, .3 miles from where you entered West Bay Street, but do not stay in the far left lane. The left turn to Fort Jackson is a mile east of the golf club.)

You will pass the Savannah Golf Club on your right, Confederate Fort Boggs was located here. Some of the earthworks have been protected by becoming part of the golf course. During the war, President Street had fortifications that lined the street from the city's outer edge to Fort Jackson.

Fort Boggs

The fortification was named for the engineer that designed it, Major William R. Boggs. Its batteries faced the south, meandering from the south and west of the outskirts of the city, along present-day 37th Street to Laurel Grove Cemetery.[51] Remnants of the fort are incorporated into the golf course at the Savannah Golf Club.

The Cotton Gin was invented in Savannah in 1793; this
machine brought economic prosperity to the South.

STOP 2:

Fort Jackson,
1 Fort Jackson Road

Construction on this fort began in 1808, but at the time of its early completion it was regarded as a battery protecting the eastern approaches to Savannah via the Savannah River.

The fort was not fully completed until the late 1850s; construction crews were still finishing up when hostilities broke out in 1861.[52]

Fort Jackson was seized by the Army of Georgia on January 10, 1861. The occupying troops were from Savannah and continued to garrison the fort as a part of the Army of Georgia until the fort was passed into control of the Confederate government.[53]

Improvements and the arming of the fort continued through the summer of 1861, and by October the fort was guarded by seven 32-pounders. Confederate troops were positioned at the fort and westward along President Street into Savannah.[54]

The fort also served as the headquarters of the Savannah River Squadron, a naval force defending the river approaches to the city. The initial fleet was formed by any vessel that could mount a gun, and was called a "mosquito fleet." Ironclads would later bolster the strength of the squadron.

Rifled artillery had breached the masonry walls at Fort Pulaski. The masonry walls at Fort Jackson are much thinner, thus reducing Jackson's defensive capabilities. A series of earthen batteries were constructed in the surrounding area to increase the defensive improvements to this strategic area.

A railroad spur was laid in 1863 to connect the fort with Savannah; the new transportation link eased the flow of troops and supplies into the area.[55]

The fort never fired a shot in anger during the war and was ordered evacuated on December 20, 1864. These troops would surrender as part of the Army of Tennessee at Durham, North Carolina, on April 26, 1865. The CSS *Georgia* was scuttled about 200 yards off of the fort on the same day, December 20.[56]

In the 1960s, the fort was owned by the Georgia Historic Commission and transferred to the Georgia Department of Natural Resources. Financial constraints almost closed the fort; however, the operation was picked by the Coastal Heritage Society.

Divers discovered the wreck of the CSS *Georgia* in 1969 and excavated two cannons. The wreck was mapped by divers in 2003 and there are plans to raise the *Georgia* in the future.

During the summer, living history programs are frequent, with daily cannon firings.

More information is available inside.

912-232-3945

www.chsgeorgia.org/jackson

Monday – Sunday, 9:00 a.m. - 5:00 p.m.

Closed Thanksgiving, Christmas, and New Years' Day.

The red buoy indicates were the CSS *Georgia* was scuttled in December 1864.

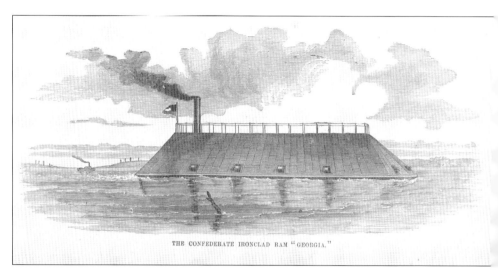

THE CONFEDERATE IRONCLAD RAM "GEORGIA."

The CSS *Georgia*, a floating battery, helped cover the evacuation into South Carolina. *Courtesy of the Coastal Heritage Society and Fort Jackson.*

Fort Jackson seen from its western approach; it
was seized by Georgia troops on January 10, 1861.

Battery Lee

This fort was built to support Fort Jackson; remnants of Battery Lee can be seen from the east wall of Fort Jackson. The fort was located on property currently owned by Kerr McGee. The fort's armament consisted of two 10-inch mortars, two 10-inch Columbiads, three 8-inch Columbiads, one 42-pound gun, one 32-pound gun, and two 24-pound Howitzers.[57]

Confederate infantry assemble for drill during a
living history program at Fort Jackson.

95

The fort's defenders march toward
the parade field for drill.

(Exit Fort Jackson and turn left back onto President Street. You are still driving east towards Fort Pulaski, about 9 miles away.)

Elba Island

Located about .5 miles east of Fort Jackson on your left is Elba Island, a Confederate signal station during the war. The bluff on your left before you cross the bridge over the Wilmington River was Battery Bartow on Caulston Bluff. Today it is a housing development.

This location served as a signal station during the war and was protected by rifle pits and the CSS *Georgia* operated here as a floating battery. Obstructions were placed from the island into the Savannah River to limit the mobility of the Union navy.[58]

The wood pylons represent all that remains of Confederate Battery Lee, built in the fall of 1861.

Battery Bartow

One of the largest forts in the Confederacy, it anchored the defense batteries that were placed in a southeasterly direction towards Rose Dew Island.[59] This fort guarded the entrance to St. Augustine Creek and the Wilmington River, both flowed into the Savannah River. General Robert E. Lee was almost killed here when a gun exploded during a test firing.[60] The fort was shelled by the Union navy in October 1862.[61]

Its armament included the following: a 10-inch Columbiad, two 24-pounders, a 12-pound rifled cannon, two 8-inch naval shell guns, two 8-inch Columbiads, two 8-pounders smoothbores, two 6-pounders smoothbores, a 3-inch rifle gun, and two 32-pounders smoothbores placed as a water battery in advance of the fort.[62]

These wooden obstacle in the water were part of the Savannah River defenses ordered by General Robert E. Lee. *Courtesy of the Coastal Heritage Society and the Savannah History Museum.*

(After crossing the bridge you will drive on a overpass to US 80 East. You will stay on this road until you reach Fort Pulaski.)

Gibson Point

This battery was located on Whitemarsh Island, near the bridge that connects Whitemarsh and Wilmington Islands. This fort protected the confluence of Richardson and Turner Creeks. A battery at Turner's Creek protected the southern end of Whitemarsh Island.[63] The forts were connected in 1864 after a Union attack against the island.

The battery was armed with two 8-inch siege howitzers and two 32-pound guns. A new defensive line was extended to Turners Point in 1864. It consisted of seven 32-pound guns and one 3-inch ordinance rifle, which protected the line that connected both forts.[64]

These gun batteries were part of Battery Bartow on Causton Bluff near St. Augustine Creek. *Courtesy of the Coastal Heritage Society and Fort Jackson.*

STOP 3:

Fort Pulaski National Monument, US 80 East

"They will make it pretty hot for you with shells, but they cannot breach your walls at that distance."[65]

General Robert E. Lee speaking to Colonel Charles Olmstead

Construction on this fort began in 1829 and was not completed until 1847 at a cost of $963,000.[66] Robert E. Lee, fresh out of West Point, engineered the drainage to allow the fort to be built on this strategic island.

On January 3, 1861, the 1st Regiment of the Army of Georgia from Savannah seized the fort. The fort had only two occupants prior to the attack, an ordinance officer and a carpenter.[67]

The fort was turned over to the Confederate States in April 1861. About 600 men were stationed at the fort during the summer; slaves and other laborers were used to repair and strengthen the fort's defenses. There were forty-eight guns that guarded the bastions.[68]

After Hilton Head fell to Union forces on November 7, 1861, General Robert E. Lee, commander of the Depart-

ment of South Carolina, Georgia, and East Florida, toured the fort and made some improvements. Ditches were dug to collect cannonballs. The ditches served two purposes, keeping cannon balls from rolling down and knocking over soldiers and capturing them for reuse.[69]

Telegraph lines between the city and Fort Pulaski were severed in February 1862. A few individuals knew the creeks well enough to move messages between Savannah and Fort Pulaski.

Union offensive preparations were complete on April 9, 1862. Gilmore ordered the Confederate commander, Colonel Charles Olmstead, to surrender, but he refused. Yankee guns opened up just after 8 a.m. on April 10.[70] Confederate return fire was inaccurate, so Gilmore ordered the concentration of all his guns to the southeast corner of the fort. A breach of the wall, Gilmore figured would force the fort to surrender. By the next afternoon, Union gunners had shells falling above the powder magazine. The magazine protected 40,000 lbs. of black powder and this forced Olmstead to ask for terms on April 11.[71] Olmstead thought a direct hit would doom his men and the fort.

Union occupation would be very boring; the fort was used as a site to exchange prisoners of war. Later in 1864, the fort was home for 600 Confederate officers who were prisoners of war.[72]

Confederate Jefferson Davis spent an evening here in May 1865, after being captured at Irwinsville. He was on his way to imprisonment at Fortress Monroe.

The fort was strengthened and modernized between 1869 and 1872. It housed German prisoners of war during World War I and became part of the National Park Service in 1933.[73] More information can be found inside, and make sure you walk around the perimeter of the fort to see some of the damage inflicted by the Union rifled artillery.
912-786-5787
www.nps.gov/fopu
Monday – Sunday, 9:00 am - 5:00 p.m.
Closed Thanksgiving and Christmas.

(After leaving Fort Pulaski, turn left on US 80 East. You will cross a bridge over the Lazaretto Creek onto Tybee Island. The next left will allow you to observe the vantage point of the Federal batteries in April 1862. The left is .3 miles from where you turned back onto US 80.)

The Georgia flag pictured was similar to the one flown by Georgia troops when they seized Fort Pulaski on January 3, 1861.

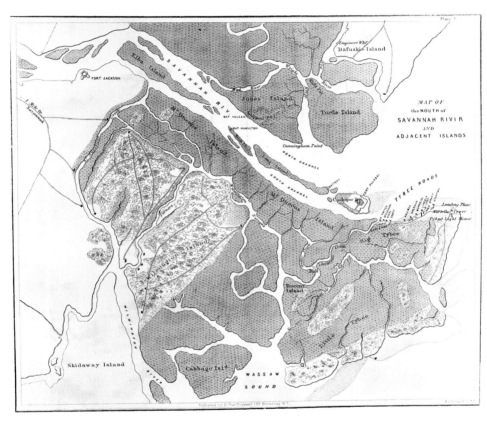

Map of Fort Pulaski and its water approaches.
Courtesy of Fort Pulaski National Monument.

Fort Pulaski was constructed in the colder
months between 1829 and 1847.

Damage is visible from the April 1862 Federal bombardment of Fort Pulaski.

The breach of the southwest corner was photographed after
the fall of Fort Pulaski on April 11, 1862. *Courtesy of Fort
Pulaski National Monument.*

The first photograph of the game of baseball was at Fort
Pulaski. The nine men behind Company K are the players.
Courtesy of Fort Pulaski National Monument.

This area was used to confine Confederate officers who were prisoners of war during the winter of 1864-65.

Shrapnel from bursting shells damaged this wall that protected the powder magazine.

The interior of the powder magazine that
was threatened by Federal artillery.

Federal officers and their wives enjoying the sun during boring garrison duty in 1863. *Courtesy of Fort Pulaski National Monument.*

Union troops on Fort Pulaski's parade ground.
Courtesy of Fort Pulaski National Monument.

STOP 4:

Federal Batteries, along the Lazaretto Creek

"unless our guns should suffer seriously from the enemy's fire, a breach would be effected...it could be seen that the rifled projectiles were surely eating their way into the scarp of the pan-coupe and adjacent south-east face."[74]

Captain Quincy Gilmore, commander of the Union guns on Tybee

Captain Quincy Gilmore quickly built batteries here to bring the fort within the range of his guns; wooden planks were used to prevent the heavy guns from sinking in the marsh mud. The batteries were strung from Goat Point, on the west side of Tybee, continuing northeasterly along the Lazaretto Creek. Roads were built linking the batteries, so it would be more efficient to move guns and ammunition during the assault. Each battery had enough powder and ordinance to fire for two days.[75]

(Turn around and take US 80 East to the Tybee Island lighthouse. Turn left at the first traffic light onto North Campell Avenue, then turn left onto Van Horne Drive, and take a right onto Meddin Drive. Park in the lot closest to the lighthouse, which is 2.6 miles from the Federal batteries.)

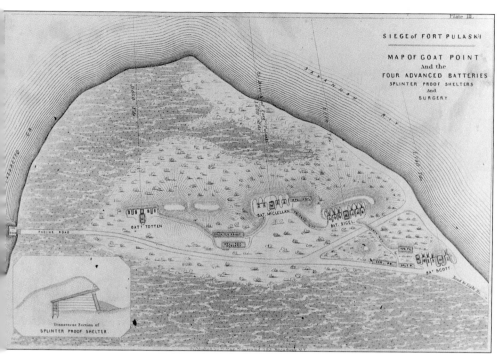

Map of Goat Point, the site of the Union batteries that attacked Fort Pulaski in April 1862. *Courtesy of Fort Pulaski National Monument.*

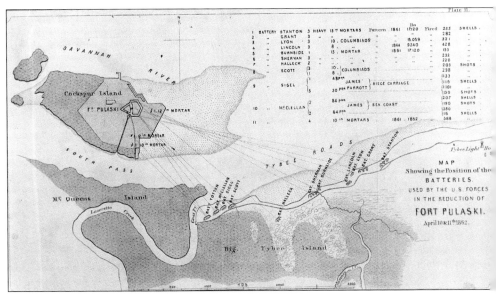

Map of the Federal batteries along Lazaretto Creek, April 1862. *Courtesy of Fort Pulaski National Monument.*

114

Union artillery bombarding Fort Pulaski, April 10, 1862. *Courtesy of Fort Pulaski National Monument.*

STOP 5:

Tybee Island Lighthouse, 30 Meddin Drive

The lighthouse that stood here at the start of the Civil War was built in 1790. The Second Assistant Keeper House was used as a barracks by Confederate troops until the evacuation of Tybee Island. During the Union occupation, it served as headquarters for the occupying force.

Early on the night of December 3, 1861, a squad of Confederate soldiers placed a keg of powder on the third story of the lighthouse, setting the woodwork and the building on fire. As they retreated, Federal gunboats began to bombard the island.[76]

More information is available inside.
912-786-5801
www.tybeelighthouse.org
April – Labor Day: Monday – Sunday, 9:00 a.m. - 6:00 p.m. Sept. – March : Monday – Sunday, 9:00 a.m. - 4:00 p.m. Closed Tuesdays and major holidays.

(Retrace your route back onto US 80 West by turning right at the light. Drive west on US 80 until it intersects with Johnny Mercer Boulevard; turn left onto this road, 7.6 miles west of the lighthouse. Johnny Mercer Boulevard merges with US 80 West, 4.9 miles up. You will turn left at the light onto US 80 West. Turner Creek is 2.6 miles from where you turned onto Johnny Mercer.)

Turner Point

This fort protected the southern end of Whitemarsh Island and was connected to Gibson Point in 1864. The armament of this battery consisted of three 10-inch Columbiads, one 20-pound Parrott gun, and two 12-pound howitzers.[77]

(After rejoining US 80 West, you will come to a bridge that spans the Wilmington River, which we crossed earlier at Causton Bluff. The bridge is 1.6 miles from the intersection of Johnny Mercer and US 80.)

As you hit the highest point on the bridge, look off to the left where the Palmer Johnson boatyard is located.

This was the general location of Fort Thunderbolt. Off to the right was a battery of guns positioned at today's Bonaventure Cemetery.

Fort Thunderbolt

"Thunderbolt is five miles to the east of Savannah and commands an important point on the Wilmington River, where there is a battery of four guns. Were Thunderbolt in our possession; we could land 20,000 men and march to Savannah over one of the finest shell roads."[78]

Philadelphia Enquirer

Blockade runners were able to bring in salt, enabling a salt-works to be established to make black powder.[79]

An attempt to break the blockade around Savannah occurred near here in the summer of 1863 when the CSS *Atlanta* tried to destroy the Union fleet in Wassaw Sound, but she ran aground and was captured.[80]

One 10-inch Columbiad, two 8-inch Columbiads, two 8-inch shell guns, one 42-pound rifle, and six 32-pound guns made up the artillery of the battery.[81]

(From the west part of the bridge, make your second right. It comes up on you quickly. Follow the road until it becomes Bonaventure Road, a mile up you will come up on the entrance of Bonaventure Cemetery.)

This revealing view from the Tybee Lighthouse
shows why the lighthouse was burned by Confederate troops in December 1861.

Tybee Island Lighthouse was
rebuilt after the war.

STOP 6:

Bonaventure Cemetery

This cemetery was opened in 1850. During the Civil War, a battery of guns was placed on the side facing the river.

Confederate generals buried here include Brigadier General George Paul Harrison, Brigadier General Robert H. Anderson, Brigadier General Alexander Lawton, and Commodore Josiah Tattnall.

(Leave the cemetery through the exit on your right and go straight. At .2 miles, turn left on Downing Drive for .6 miles, until it intersects with US 80 West, and make a right turn. Continue on US 80 West until it intersects with Skidaway Road, 2.5 miles from the bridge. You will turn left on Skidaway Road for 4.5 miles to Wormsloe.)

In the distance on the point was a Confederate battery, now Bonaventure Cemetery.

This monument stands on the approximate location of the Bonaventure Battery.

STOP 7:

Wormsloe State Historic Site, 7601 Skidaway Road

This property was first settled in 1739 by Noble Jones, who completed his house in 1745. The property was pretty much abandoned from 1745 until 1828, when Noble's son George built the existing house on the property.

During the Civil War, Confederate earthworks, Fort Wimberly, were erected along the Back River. Union troops occupied the fort in December 1864 and the house was vandalized by the soldiers. There is no access to these earthworks.

There is more information available inside.
912-353-3023
www.gaparks.org/info/wormsloe
Tuesday – Saturday, 9:00 a.m. - 5:00 p.m.
Sunday, 2:00 pm - 5:30 p.m.
Closed Mondays, Thanksgiving, Christmas, and New Year's Day.

(Turn left onto Skidaway and drive until it intersects with the Parkersburg Road and turn right. Drive .7 miles and veer to the left onto Cornius Drive. The church will be on your left. Pull into the parking lot.)

The oaks lead to Wormsloe Plantation, site of a
Confederate battery during the war.

STOP 8:

Isle of Hope United Methodist Church

The Church was constructed in 1859 and it served as a hospital for the Confederate troops that were stationed here. Thirty soldiers from nearby Effingham County are buried here.

This battery was armed with two 8-inch Columbiads and five 32-pounders. Soldiers from nearby garrisoned this area along the Skidaway River.[82]

(Turn back onto Cornius, heading back to the Parkersburg Road, turn left onto Ferguson Avenue, 1.2 miles.)

Bethesda

This was a home for boys, but the boys were evacuated to Jefferson County. Bethesda became a hospital for Confederate soldiers stationed in the area. The original home was established in 1740. None of the original buildings survive. The school is still open.

The museum is open Monday through Friday, 9:00 a.m. - 5:00 p.m.

(Continue on Ferguson for 2.4 miles and turn left on Georgia Spur 204. Follow the spur for 2.8 miles to Skidaway State Park.)

The Isle of Hope Methodist Church was built in 1859 and was the site of a Confederate battery during the war.

Confederate dead from nearby Effingham County are buried in the church's grave yard.

STOP 9:

Skidaway Island State Park

This battery was constructed by Georgia troops in the spring of 1861; it had ten guns with bomb-proofs and trenches. A bomb-proof was an earthen shelter in which soldiers could hide during a bombardment.

The Georgia Hussars garrisoned the island until June 1861. Union naval vessels, numbering about twenty, were anchored off the Skidaway batteries by February 1862 and the fort was abandoned in March when supply became too difficult. The guns were moved to Thunderbolt and Beaulieu.[83]
www.gaparks.org/info/Skidaway

(Turn right on Georgia Spur 204 West and drive 2.4 miles to Ferguson Avenue, turning right. Continue on Ferguson for 2.7 miles, until it intersects with Skidaway Road. Follow Skidaway for 3.8 miles until it intersects with Victory Drive, US 80. Turn left onto US 80 West. Follow US 80 or Victory Drive 2.3 miles to Drayton Street and turn right. Follow Drayton until you cross 37th Street, .3 miles, turn left onto 37th Street for 1 mile, turn right onto the Ogeechee Road for .5 miles, and turn left onto Anderson Street. You have arrived at Laurel Grove Cemetery.)

Skidaway Island – Confederate troops occupied the island
until March 1862, when supply became difficult. These
earthworks are the remnants of that occupation.

STOP 10:

Laurel Grove Cemetery, 802 West Anderson Street

"To the Confederate Dead. To the Men of Gettysburg."

The Gettysburg monument in Laurel Grove Cemetery

This cemetery opened in 1853. Over 600 Confederate dead are buried here. Plots were dedicated to the Confederate war dead around the Gettysburg monument in 1875. Confederate generals buried here include Brigadier General Gilbert Moxley Sorrel, Major General Lafayette McLaws, Brigadier General Francis S. Bartow, Brigadier General Henry Rootes Jackson, and Brigadier General Jeremy Francis Gilmer. Anna Mitchell Davenport is also buried here; she was a co-founder of the United Daughters of the Confederacy. There is also a monument here for the United Daughters of the Confederacy.

(To complete the tour, drive out onto Anderson Street until it intersects with Martin Luther King Boulevard, turn left for .9 miles to the Round House Museum, where the tour ends.)

This plot honors Savannahians killed on July 2, 1863, during the Battle of Gettysburg.

"Silence for her Sons," at the Gettysburg monument, was placed here in 1875.

Chapter 4
Siege of Savannah, December 1864 Driving Tour

(This tour will start at the Round House Museum, at the intersection of West Harris Street and Martin Luther King Jr. Boulevard. Please enter the museum. There are Civil War era ruins and buildings here.)

STOP 1:

Round House Museum, 601 West Harris Street

The round house was owned by the Central of Georgia Railroad. The railroad was completed in 1842, linking Savannah with Macon. At the time it was the longest railroad in the world. The line helped move cotton to the port of Savannah. The machine shops were constructed here in 1853; the preexisting shops of the Central of Georgia Railroad had been destroyed by a fire in 1851.[84] In 1861, the repair shops were used to finish gun mounts for local defense and were contracted out by other Confederate states for that same reason. The never-ending de-

mands for gun mounts forced the Central of Georgia to construct new repair shops in Macon in 1863. Sherman destroyed all the locomotives and rolling stock in Savannah, but the repair shops were spared so that the Union Navy could use the shops to repair some of its ships. Many of the roofs of the existing shops were destroyed by Hurricane David in 1979. The museum is now a National Historic Landmark.
912-651-6823
www.chsgeorgia.org
Open daily, 9:00 a.m. - 5:00 pm everyday.

(After leaving the Round House Museum, turn left onto Martin Luther King Boulevard and make your next left onto the Louisville Road.)

Smoke stack built in 1853, from the Round House Museum.

These repair shops built gun carriages for the Confederacy.

Louisville Road was used by retreating Confederate troops who were evacuating the western defenses and by General Geary's column as it marched into Savannah in December 1864.

(Traveling along the Louisville Road, it will intersect with Stiles Avenue on the left, .9 miles)

This intersection is the site where Savannah's Mayor, Dr. Richard Arnold, surrendered the city to General John Geary.

(Continue on the Louisville Road through the overpass, 1.3 miles, and turn left on Telfair Road. Follow Telfair Road until it intersects with the Chatham Parkway, 2.5 miles.)

Telfair Road parallels the western Confederate defenses. The road was used by retreating Confederate troops and advancing Union troops on December 20-21, 1864.

The junction where Telfair Road and Chatham Parkway intersect was the scene of some heavy fighting on December 10. The school in front of you was part of Daly's Farm in 1864. Two Union attacks were launched against this position and were repeatedly repulsed; they were trying to take the earthworks that protected a causeway over the canal. The Confederates were using the Savannah and Ogeechee Canal as their line of defense, stretching north to south linking the Savannah and Ogeechee Rivers. The Confederates evacuated these positions on December 20.

(Turn left onto Chatham Parkway and make the next right onto Interstate 16 West for 2 miles. Exit off I-16 and the Dean Forest Road, Georgia Route 307. Turn left on 307 and travel down this road until it intersects with US Route 17, 2.5 miles.)

The road that you are now on parallels with Sherman's battle lines during the Siege of Savannah. The marshy land on both sides of the road was part of the Silk Hope Rice Plantation in 1864.

(Turn left onto US 17 North, travel .4 miles, and turn left into the Salt Creek Boat Ramp.)

Federals attacking at Daly's Farm. They were thrown back twice.

STOP 2:

Salt Creek Boat Ramp, Battery Jones

Battery Jones, a Confederate fortification, occupied this ground in December 1864. This battery was made up of two 32-pounder garrison guns, one 32-pounder carronade, one 20-pounder parrot, and four 12-pounder Napoleons. This battery saw heavy shelling during the siege on December 10. Union guns were amassed on the other side of the creek.[85] Another battery occupied the area on the other side of US 17, Pine Point. The old causeway for the Old Silk Road is on your left, the bridge that is blocked.

Pine Point
This battery supported Battery Jones with six field pieces.[86]

(Leave the boat ramp by turning right onto US 17 South.)

This area had many rice plantations during the war. The creeks provided water for the area's then rice culture. Dams and dykes were constructed from the tidal creeks to the rice fields to regulate the flow of water during high tide. General Hardee destroyed this irrigation system before the siege, so that there was standing water between three and six feet. This made these areas impassable to Union troops trying to advance through the rice fields.[87] The other plantations that were along this road in 1864 were the Lebanon and Berwyck Plantations. The destruction of these dams and dykes caused the rice culture in the area to pass into history.

(Continue on US 17 South for 3.1 miles to King's Ferry or to the King's Bridge Boat Ramp that will be on your left.)

US 17 now travels along the Old Savannah-Darien Road, linking Savannah, Darien, and Brunswick. This road was used extensively by Sherman's troops as they maneuvered around Savannah. The 15th and 17th Corps of the Union's Army of the Tennessee established their headquarters along this road.

(Turn left at the next boat ramp that comes into view as you get close to the Ogeechee River.)

Battery Jones, along Salt Creek, was part of the Confederate defenses.

The 32-pounder gun was part of the defenses here; this gun is on display at Fort McAllister.

STOP 3:

King's Bridge, King's Ferry in 1864, over the Ogeechee River

In 1862 this could have provided the Union a foothold that allowed their troops to march twelve miles to Savannah without meeting any resistance. A strong Union naval threat in the summer of 1862 forced the Confederates to build Fort McAllister, about 10 miles down river from here. It protected the entrance to the Ogeechee River.

Further up the river, the important railroad bridges of the Savannah, Albany & Gulf were potential targets to the Union navy.

The original bridge during the war was destroyed by retreating Confederates in December 1864. On December 9, Union cavalry scouts from here canoed down the river past Fort McAllister to make contact with the Union Navy to inform them of Sherman's presence in the area.

After the fall of Fort McAllister, Sherman had docks and wharfs built here in order to receive supplies from the Union Navy.

(Leave by driving under the overpass to the restaurant and right back onto US 17 South, continue on 17 until it intersects with Georgia Route 144, turn left onto 144 East. You are now driving to Fort McAllister.)

Richmond Hill was known as Ways Station during the war.

King's Bridge over the Ogeechee River where
Sherman made contact with the Union navy.

Union cavalry scouts floated down the Ogeechee to
make the initial contact with the navy.

STOP 4:

Fort McAllister State Historic Site

"They took it Howard. I've got Savannah."[88]

General William T. Sherman on the capture of the fort, December 13, 1864

This area was known was Genesis Point in the summer of 1861, when a battery of guns was constructed here to protect the twelve cotton and rice plantations that flourished along the Ogeechee River and the vital railroad bridge that was located upriver.[89]

The area was considered the back door to Savannah, anchoring the southern flank of Savannah's river defenses. The battery that was positioned here was operational by September 1861. The garrison was trained in both infantry and heavy artillery tactics.[90]

Obstructions and torpedoes were placed in the river in the spring of 1862 to prevent Union naval movements upriver.[91] The fort was enlarged and renamed Fort McAllister in June 1862. A cavalry rear guard protected the land entrance to the fort.[92]

War found Fort McAllister in July 1862, when the CSS *Nashville*, a blockade runner,

was trying to elude the Union navy by steaming up the Ogeechee and finding protection under the guns of Fort McAllister.[93]

The Union Navy attacked Fort McAllister seven times between July 1862 and March 1863, never able to take the fort by water. They were, however, able to catch up and destroy the *Nashville* in February 1863. The fort was able to survive because the shells were absorbed into the walls and detonation did not cause much structural damage.

Some of these attacks were used to test the Union monitors against land-based artillery.

Fort McAllister would remain quiet until December 1864, when Sherman's army approached the city. By 1864, much of the fort's manpower had been ordered elsewhere, but more artillery had been added.[94]

As Sherman's troops approached the city, Major Gen-

140

eral Oliver Howard's Right Wing, about 30,000 strong, was approaching the fort. At this time, Fort McAllister had 235 men. The fort was the only obstacle between Howard and the sea.

The defenders had placed land torpedoes on the land approach to the fort. It was hoped that these mines would slow the advance of a Union attack. A Confederate picket had been captured and alerted the attackers.[95]

Sherman ordered Brigadier General William B. Hazen's 2nd Division, 4000 men, to attack the fort. These veterans had served since Shiloh. The attack was ordered for late afternoon on December 13, skirmishers exchanged fire while the torpedoes were being removed. Hazen then ordered three brigades towards the fort. The fire intensified as the skirmishers had a far-reaching impact on the Confederate artillerymen.[96]

Within twenty minutes of the attack, the fort had been overrun and was in Union hands.[97] The Union Army now controlled the Ogeechee River and Ossabaw Sound, so supplies were now able to flow freely. After the battle the Union troops used the Confederate prisoners to locate the torpedoes and later moved all of the heavy artillery from the fort.[98]

Henry Ford began to restore the fort in the 1930s, but his work ended in 1945 when he suffered a stroke. International Paper deeded the fort to the state of Georgia in 1958, which was placed under the care of the Georgia Department of Natural Resources.

Today the site is active in preserving the area's Civil War history through interpretive programs and living histories. A long-term project is the complete salvage of the *Nashville*. Close to 150,000 visitors tour the fort each year. A living history or reenactment is scheduled for the second weekend in December.[99]

There is more information available inside.
912-727-2339
twww.fortmcallister.org
Tuesday – Saturday, 9:00 a.m. - 5:00 p.m.
Sunday, 2:00 pm - 5:00 p.m.
Closed Mondays, Thanksgiving, and Christmas

(Retrace your path back down 144 West to the intersection with US 17, turn right onto US 17 North, continue on 17 until it intersects with Georgia Route 204. Turn left on 204 West, travel 3.2 miles to the Savannah and Ogeechee Canal.)

Abatis helped protect Fort McAllister from a land assault.

Confederate prisoners being gathered by Union troops.

Union troops on walls, guarding Confederate prisoners of war.

Earthen walls at Fort McAllister, along the Ogeechee River.

The parade ground inside Fort McAllister.

Confederate 32-pounder guarding the fort against naval attacks.

STOP 5:

Savannah and Ogeechee Canal, 681 Fort Argyle Road

The canal was constructed to link the Savannah and Ogeechee Rivers; the sixteen and a half mile man made waterway was built between 1824 and 1830. The canal allowed cotton, rice, and lumber to reach the port of Savannah and then travel onward to the outside world.[100]

During the war, service was not interrupted until Sherman's army approached Savannah. In 1864, the canal helped shape the Confederate western line of defense. Union troops tried to cross the canal at Shaw's Bridge, lock number 3, on December 8. They were twice thrown back.

Where you are located, Confederate defenders burned Dillon's Bridge over the Ogeechee River, near lock number 6. This lock is located on these grounds. Union General Corse found the bridge in flames when he arrived in force. A pontoon bridge was quickly laid on December 10.[101]

Union General Smith's division of the 15th Corps crossed further up the Ogeechee at Fort Argyle, cutting the canal.[102]

The canal suffered $22,000 in damages from the war and was closed for months; the banks had been cut by the Confederates to flood the surrounding rice fields. Repairs were not completed until 1866.

The canal operated until 1891, when it could no longer compete with the railroads.[103] 912-748-8068 www.socanalmuseum.com Monday – Sunday, 9:00 a.m. - 5:00 p.m.

148

(Retrace your drive on 204, but heading east this time until it intersects with Interstate 95. Take I-95 North until it intersects with I-16, about 5 miles. Turn right onto I-16 East, heading towards Savannah. Stay on 16 for 2.5 miles and exit onto Georgia Route 307, turn left. Stay on 307 until it intersects with US Route 80, turn right at the light onto 80 East.)

You will approach an overpass over some railroad tracks, 2.5 miles from the intersection with 307. This railroad line was part of the Central of Georgia during the war. General Sherman was almost killed here by Confederate artillery fire.

Battery McBeth

This battery had three 32-pound guns on barbette carriages and two 24-pounder Blakely rifle guns on siege carriages. This battery fired the shot that almost killed General Sherman.[104]

(Follow 80 until it intersects with US 17 North and Georgia Route 25 – 17 and 25 are the same road. You will see a street sign, Burnsed Avenue, turn left here at the light.)

About .3 miles up on 17 & 25 you will cross over the Dundee Canal, part of the Confederate defense line. They used the canal to help flood the surrounding area.

As you continue north you come into an area that was occupied by the Colerain Plantation during the war.

(Continue on 17 North into Port Wentworth to the landing before the Houlihan Bridge.)

Lock 5 of the Savannah-Ogeechee Canal.

The canal stretched 16.5 miles between the Savannah and Ogeechee Rivers.

STOP 6:

Houlihan Bridge Boat Landing, US 17 North along the Savannah River

North 1.5 miles from the landing is Argyle Island, where the 3rd Wisconsin Infantry maneuvered to try and get to the South Carolina side of the Savannah River. It was tough with all the rice fields that were here during the war. Fighting erupted on December 15, when Federal troops were trying to squeeze the western defenses along the Savannah River.

(Return to 17, once you cross the second bridge you are now on Argyle Island. Be careful if you care to stop, for there is no shoulder. Continue until you cross into South Carolina and turn right onto US 17 Alternate South, .32 miles, you are now heading back towards Savannah.)

Skirmishing occurred here with Wheeler's Confederate Cavalry and the 3rd Wisconsin, Wheeler was screening the evacuation of Savannah.

(Continue on 17 South to the bridge over the Savannah River and end the tour at the Savannah Visitors Center.)

Argyle Island – Union troops tried to use this island as a spring-board to cut off the Confederate evacuation of Savannah.

STOP 7:

Savannah Visitor Center and History Museum

Monday through Friday from
8:30 a.m. - 5:00 p.m.
Saturday and Sunday, 9:00
a.m. - 5:00 p.m.

TOUR ENDS

Irish Jasper Greens Monument in the Catholic Cemetery.

Endnotes

1. Lawrence, Alexander A. *A Present for Mr. Lincoln* (Savannah, GA: The Oglethorpe Press, Inc. 1997) 210.
2. *Ibid,* 210.
3. *Ibid,* 214.
4. Anderson, Edward C. *Confederate Foreign Agent: The European Diary of Major Edward C. Anderson*. Ed. W. Stanley Hode (University of Alabama: Confederate Publishing Co, 1976) 9.
5. Anderson, 3.
6. *Ibid.*
7. Bell, Derek. *Civil War Savannah* (Savannah, GA: Frederic C. Bell, Inc. 1997) 15.
8. Durham , Roger S. "Savannah: Mr. Lincoln's Christmas Present." *Blue & Gray Magazine* February 1991, 11.
9. Ibid, 44.
10. Guss, John, site manager at Fort Jackson. Personal interview with David D'Arcy, 8 June 2004.
11. Bell, 10.
12. Lawrence, 148.
13. Durham, 11.
14. Lawrence, 148.
15. Ibid, 233.
16. Ibid, 226.
17. Lawrence, 32.
18. Ibid, 243
19. Ibid, 243.
20. Ibid, 21.
21. Sorrel, G. Moxley. *At the Right-hand of Longstreet: Recollections of a Confederate Staff Officer* (University of Nebraska Press: Lincoln & London, 1999) 232.
22. Ibid, 202.
23. Anderson, 48.
24. Ibid, 39.
25. Bell, 58.
26. Lawrence, 273.
27. Ibid, 135.
28. Berendt, John. *Midnight in the Garden of Good and Evil* (New York: Random House, 1994) 367.
29. Lawrence, 213.
30. Anderson, 25.
31. Ibid, 212.
32. Ibid.
33. Anderson, 71.
34. Ibid, 78.
35. Ibid, 57.
36. Ibid, 58.
37. Bell, 53.
38. Ibid.
39. Yates Pember, Phoebe. *A Southern Woman's Story: Life in Confederate Richmond*. Ed. Bell Irvin Wiley (Jackson, Tennessee: McCovat-Mercer Press Inc., 1959) 131.
40. Bell, 266.
41. Ibid, 267.
42. Ibid.
43. Alexander, Edward Porter. *Fighting for the Confederacy. The Personal Recollections of General Edward Porter Alexander*. Ed. Gary W. Gallagher. (Chapel Hill/London: The University of North Carolina Press, 1989) 310.
44. Ibid, 259.
45. Ibid, 255.
46. Ibid, 257.
47. Ibid.
48. Sherman, 730.
49. *Savannah Daily Morning News*, 15 November 1859.
50. Jones, Charles C. *The Siege of Savannah in December, 1864 and the Confederate Operations in Georgia and the Third Military of South Carolina during General Sherman's March from Atlanta to the Sea.* Albany, 1874. <http://www.civilwarhistory.com/101899/siegeofsavannah/savannah.html. Jones, 101.
51. Byous, Jim. *The Fortresses of Savannah.* <http://www.sip.armstrong.edu/forts/essays.html. >

52. Guss interview.
53. Ibid.
54. Ibid.
55. Ibid.
56. Sherman, William Tecumseh. *Memoirs of General W. T. Sherman*, (New York: Library Classics of the United States of America, 1990) 722.
57. Jones, 102.
58. Guss interview.
59. Guss interview.
60. Jones, 81.
61. Guss interview.
62. Jones, 102.
63. Byous.
64. Jones, 103.
65. Bell, 62.
66. *Savannah Daily Morning News,* 20 January 1861.
67. Kirkland, Tally. Site manager at Fort Pulaski. Personal interview with David D'Arcy. 30 April 2004.
68. Kirkland interview.
69. Gillmore, Brig. Gen Q. A. *Siege and Reduction of Fort Pulaski.* (Gettysburg, 1988) 24
70. Latimore, Ralston B. *Fort Pulaski National Monument.* (Washington DC, 1954) 24.
71. Kirkland interview.
72. Latimore, 38.
73. Ibid, 43.
74. Bell, 77.
(***Please provide the endnote citation for 75. Thanks.**)
76. *Savannah Daily Morning News,* 5 December 1861.
77. Jones, 103.
78. *Philadelphia Enquirer,* 7 February 1862.
79. Thunderbolt Museum.
80. Byous.
81. Jones, 103.
82. Jones, 103.
83. Byous.
84. *Savannah Daily Morning News,* 17 July 1856.
85. Jones, 84.
86. Ibid.
87. Christman, William E. *Undaunted: The History of Fort McAllister* (Georgia Department of Resources, 1996) 62.
88. Davis, Burke. *Sherman's March* (New York: Vintage Books, 1980) 105.
89. Brown, Daniel, site manager at Fort McAllister. Personal interview with David D'Arcy. 29 July 2004.
90. Christman, 7.
91. Ibid, 10.
92. Ibid.
93. Ibid, 12.
94. Ibid, 70.
95. Sherman, 262.
96. Christman, 65.
97. Ibid, 70.
98. Davis, 105.
99. Brown interview.
100. Chica Arndt, director of Savannah-Ogeechee Canal. Personal interview with David D'Arcy. 25 August 2004.
101. Ibid.
102. Georgia State Plaque, Jab025-72, 1959.
103. Arndt interview.
104. Jones, 82.

Bibliography

Alexander, Edward Porter. *Fighting for the Confederacy. The Personal Recollections of General Edward Porter Alexander.* Ed. Gary W. Gallagher. Chapel Hill/London: The University of North Carolina Press, 1989.

Anderson, Edward C. *Confederate Foreign Agent: The European Diary of Major Edward C. Anderson.* Ed. W. Stanley Hode. University of Alabama: Confederate Publishing Co., 1976.

Arndt, Chica. Director of Savannah-Ogeechee Canal, personal interview with David D'Arcy, 25 August 2004

Bell, Derek. *Civil War Savannah.* Savannah, Georgia: Frederic C. Bell Inc., 1997.

Berendt, John. *Midnight in the Garden of Good and Evil.* New York: Random House, 1994.

Brown, Daniel. Site manager at Fort McAllister, personal interview with David D'Arcy, 29 July 2004.

Byous, Jim. *The Fortresses of Savannah.* <http://www.sip.armstrong.edu/forts/essays.html>.

Christman, William E. *Undaunted: The History of Fort McAllister.* Georgia Department of Resources, 1996.

Davis, Burke. *Sherman's March.* New York: Vintage Books, 1980.

Denkin, Stephen R. "Politics and Sectionalism in the 1850s." <http://odur.let.rugnl/usa/E/1850s/poli4.htm.>.

Durham, Roger S. "Savannah: Mr. Lincoln's Christmas Present." *Blue & Gray Magazine*, February 1991.

Gillmore, Brig. Gen Q. A. *Siege and Reduction of Fort Pulaski.* Gettysburg, 1988.

Guss, John. Site manager at Fort Jackson, personal interview with David D'Arcy, 8 June 2004.

Jones, Charles C. *The Siege of Savannah in December, 1864 and the Confederate Operations in Georgia and the Third Military of South Carolina during General Sherman's March from Atlanta to the Sea.* Albany, 1874. <http://www.civilwarhistory.com/101899/siegeofsavannah/savannah.html.>.

Kirkland, Tally. Site manager at Fort Pulaski, personal interview with David D'Arcy, 30 April 2004.

Laltimore, Ralston B. *Fort Pulaski National Monument.* Washington D.C., 1954

Lawrence, Alexander A. *A Present for Mr. Lincoln.* Savannah, Georgia: The Oglethorpe Press, Inc., 1997.

McMurry, Richard. "On the Road to the Sea, Sherman's Savannah Campaign." *Civil War Times,* Vol. XXI, January 1983.

Oeffinger, John C., Ed. *A Soldier's General: The Civil War Letters of Major General Lafayette McLaws.* University of North Carolina Press, 2002.

Philadelphia Enquirer, 7 February 1862.

Savannah Daily Morning News, 17 July 1856.

Savannah Daily Morning News, 15 November 1859.

Savannah Daily Morning News, 20 January 1861.

Savannah Daily Morning News, 5 December 1861

Sherman, William Tecumseh.

Memoirs of General W. T. Sherman. New York: Library Classics of the United States of America, 1990.

Sorrel, G. Moxley. *At the Right-hand of Longstreet: Recollections of a Confederate Staff Officer.* Lincoln & London: University of Nebraska Press, 1999.

Wortham, Karen. First African Baptist Church Historian, interview with David D'Arcy, 9 June 2004.

Yates Pember, Phoebe. *A Southern Woman's Story: Life in Confederate Richmond.* Ed. Bell Irvin Wiley. Jackson, Tennessee: McCovat-Mercer Press Inc., 1959.